Bony-skinned Dinosaurs

Robin Birch

CHELSEA CLUBHOUSE

An Imprint of Chelsea House Publishers

This edition published in 2009 in the United States of America by Chelsea Clubhouse, an imprint of Chelsea House Publishers.

Chelsea Clubhouse
An imprint of Chelsea House Publishers
132 West 31st Street
New York, NY 10001

Chelsea Clubhouse books are available at special discounts when purchased in bulk quantities for businesses, associations, institutions, or sales promotions. Please call our Special Sales Department in New York at (212) 967-8800 or (800) 322-8755.

You can find Chelsea Clubhouse on the World Wide Web at: http://www.chelseahouse.com

First published in 2002 by
MACMILLAN EDUCATION AUSTRALIA PTY LTD
15–19 Claremont Street, South Yarra, 3141

Visit our Web site at www.macmillan.com.au or go directly to www.macmillanlibrary.com.au

Associated companies and representatives throughout the world.

Copyright © Robin Birch 2009; 2002
Library of Congress Cataloging-in-Publication Data
Birch, Robin.
    Bony-skinned dinosaurs / by Robin Birch.
    p. cm. — (Dinosaur world)
    Includes index.
    Summary: Describes the appearance, eating habits, and habitat of bony-skinned dinosaurs, including Stegosaurus, Kentrosaurus, Ankylosaurus, Sauropelta, and Panoplosaurus.
    ISBN 978-1-60413-404-9
    1. Ornithischia—Juvenile literature. [1. Ornithischians. 2. Dinosaurs.] I. Title. II. Series.
    QE862.O65 B57 2009
    567.914—dc21

                                                                        2008000845

Edited by Angelique Campbell-Muir
Illustrations by Nina Sanadze
Page layout by Nina Sanadze

Printed in the United States of America

Acknowledgements

Department of Library Services, American Museum of Natural History (neg. no. PK51), p. 9; Auscape/ James L. Amos & Peter Arnold, p. 5, Auscape/Parer & Parer-Cook, p. 13; © The Natural History Museum, London, pp. 8 (bottom), 12, 16; Getty Images/Photodisc, p. 24; Royal Tyrrell Museum of Palaeontology/Alberta Community Development, pp. 8 (top), 29.

Contents

Glossary words

When a word is printed in **bold**, you can look up its meaning in the Glossary on page 31.

Dinosaurs

Many different kinds of dinosaurs once roamed the earth. They lived millions of years ago.

There were many different kinds of dinosaurs.

Scientists have dug up bones from the ground and studied them. They have put the bones together to make **skeletons**. From these skeletons, we can learn how dinosaurs looked and how they lived.

Dinosaur skeletons are often kept in museums.

Bony Skins

Some dinosaurs had hard bone on the outside of their skin. These bony-skinned dinosaurs ate plants.

Some bony-skinned dinosaurs ate ferns in forests.

Some of the bone made small bumps on the dinosaurs' skin. Scientists have found some skin **fossils** buried in the ground.

This fossil shows the shape of a bony-skinned dinosaur's skin.

Some bony-skinned dinosaurs had **spikes** and some had **plates**. Some of these larger bones stuck up in the air and some lay flat on the skin.

spike

plate

This bony-skinned dinosaur has plates on its back.

Spikes and plates helped bony-skinned dinosaurs defend themselves against attacks by meat-eating dinosaurs.

bony skin

This bony-skinned dinosaur is being attacked by two meat-eating dinosaurs.

Stegosaurus
(STEG-uh-SAWR-uhs)

Stegosaurus had a large body and a very small head. It had large, triangle-shaped plates that ran in two rows the length of its back. It also had four long spikes at the end of its tail.

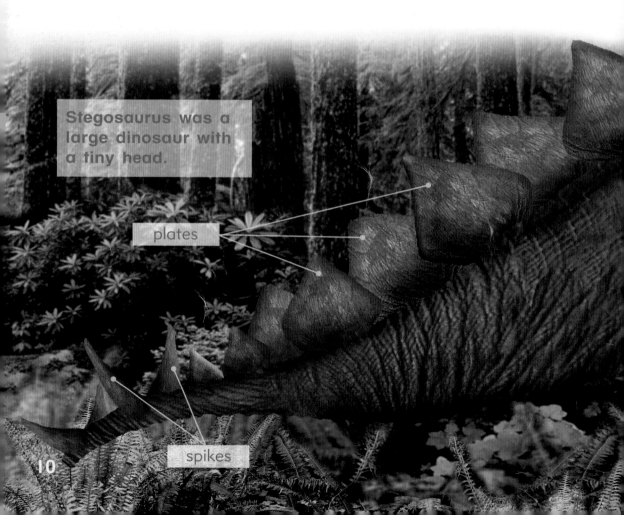

Stegosaurus was a large dinosaur with a tiny head.

plates

spikes

Stegosaurus walked on four heavy legs. Its back legs were longer and straighter than its front legs. Its front feet had five wide toes, and its back feet had three wide toes.

small head

Stegosaurus had a narrow beak and small, weak teeth in its cheeks. It probably ate leaves, shoots, and other soft plants. It found its food in the **woodlands** where it lived.

The bones of the Stegosaurus show it had a small head and a narrow beak.

Stegosaurus could swing its spiky tail from side to side to fight other dinosaurs.

Stegosaurus used its tail spikes to protect itself against other dinosaurs.

Kentrosaurus

(KEN-truh-SAWR-uhs)

Kentrosaurus was not a very big dinosaur. It measured 17 feet (5 meters) long. Its head was small compared to its body.

plates

long side spike

14

Kentrosaurus had small plates on its neck and larger plates on its back. Long spikes ran down its hips and tail. A longer spike stuck out of each side of its body.

spikes

Kentrosaurus was not a very large dinosaur.

Kentrosaurus lived in warm, damp areas near rivers. It ate ferns and other low-growing plants. It bit off plants with its beak.

Kentrosaurus ate plants such as ferns.

The dinosaur's back legs were twice as long as its front legs. Sometimes Kentrosaurus may have stood on its back legs and rested on its tail to reach leaves in high places.

Kentrosaurus may have used its tail to balance when reaching for food.

Ankylosaurus

(ang-KY-luh-SAWR-uhs)

Ankylosaurus was a huge, bulky dinosaur. It measured as long as 35 feet (11 meters).

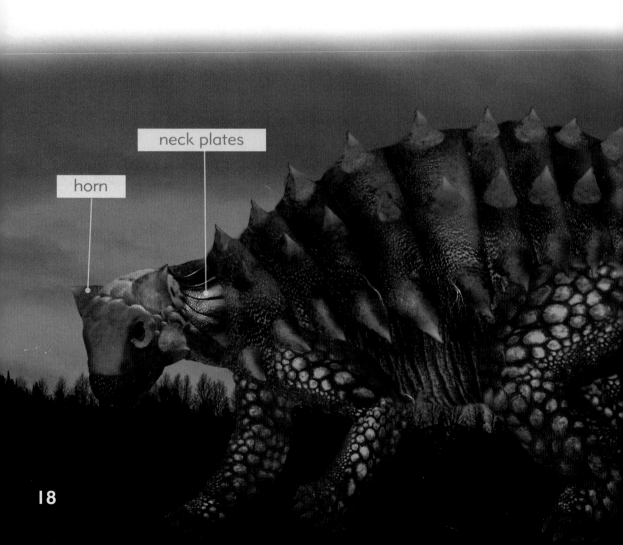

horn

neck plates

Bony plates and rows of spikes covered the top part of the dinosaur's body. Ankylosaurus also had horns on its head. Only its underbelly did not have plates.

club made of bone

spikes

Ankylosaurus was a large, heavy dinosaur.

Ankylosaurus had a heavy club at the end of its stiff tail. The club was solid bone. Ankylosaurus could swing its tail for protection if attacked by a meat-eating dinosaur. The club probably could have broken a big dinosaur's leg.

tail club

This Ankylosaurus is fighting off a meat-eating dinosaur with its tail club.

Ankylosaurus is called an armored dinosaur because its plates and spikes cover most of its body. People used to wear armor in battles to protect themselves.

People used to wear armor such as this to protect themselves in battles.

Sauropelta

(SAWR-oh-PEL-tah)

Sauropelta was an armored dinosaur. It had bony bumps on its head, back, and tail. Only its underbelly was not armored.

long spikes

soft underbelly

Sauropelta had long spikes on its neck and short spikes all the way down its sides and tail.

short spikes

Sauropelta was not a very large dinosaur.

Sauropelta may have crouched down when a meat-eating dinosaur attacked to protect its soft underside. Sauropelta had to rely on its armor for protection.

armor

This Sauropelta is crouching down to protect its soft belly.

Scientists have found some of Sauropelta's skin and armor. These fossils show the dinosaur's bony bumps.

This fossil shows the shape of Sauropelta's skin.

Panoplosaurus

(pan-OP-luh-SAWR-uhs)

At 23 feet (7 meters) long, Panoplosaurus was one of the smaller armored dinosaurs. Bumps, plates, and spikes covered most of its body.

thick plates

Panoplosaurus had thick plates on its shoulders. Rows of bony bumps ran down its back and stiff tail. Spikes protected its sides.

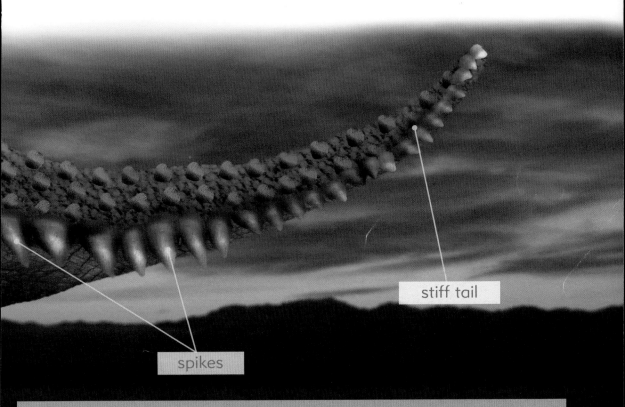

stiff tail

spikes

Panoplosaurus was quite small for a bony-skinned dinosaur.

Panoplosaurus had a pear-shaped head with a narrow beak. It could reach into small areas to find the softest and juiciest plants to eat. It also had teeth in its cheeks to grind tougher leaves and twigs.

narrow beak

Panoplosaurus used its narrow beak to reach plants.

Panoplosaurus probably used its long shoulder spikes for protection against meat-eating dinosaurs. It may have used them to stab a **predator's** feet and legs.

Panoplosaurus used its shoulder spikes to protect itself.

Names and Their Meanings

"Dinosaur" means "terrible lizard."

"Stegosaurus" means "roof lizard."

"Kentrosaurus" means "spiked lizard."

"Ankylosaurus" means "**fused** lizard."

"Sauropelta" means "lizard **shield**."

"Panoplosaurus" means "armored lizard."

Glossary

bulky   to be large and take up a lot of space

club   a thick, heavy stick used as a weapon; some bony-skinned dinosaurs had a club-like tail.

fossil   something left behind by a plant or animal that has been preserved in the earth; examples are dinosaur bones and footprints.

fused   joined together

plate   a flat piece of bone that forms part of an animal's body

predator   an animal that hunts other animals for food

shield   a piece of armor for protection

skeleton   the bones that support and protect an animal's body

spike   a pointed piece of bone on a dinosaur's body

stiff   does not bend

woodland   land covered mainly by trees

Index